Womanish Breaths

*Womanist micropoetry that affirms & uplifts the concert of Divinity & **BLACK** Womanhood.*

Written By: ORIT

Womanish Breaths

*Womanist micropoetry that affirms & uplifts the concert of Divinity & **BLACK** Womanhood.*

Written By: ORIT

Ruach & Emet Publishing

Copyright © 2016 by ORIT
All rights reserved.
ISBN: 069277131X
ISBN-13: 978-0692771310
Ruach & Emet Publishing, Delaware, Ohio

DEDICATIONS

Thank You CREATOR-YESHUA-GREAT SPIRIT… In every Manifestation you express yourself… Thank you for breathing into me and allowing me to become a living soul. May I fulfill my duty in this life….Ashe'!

To Korryn Gaines, I didn't know you personally, but your winds blow on me…Thank you for exemplifying to us that we have a right to live free; I honor you, dear sister of ours… You are a powerful & proud BLACK Woman, now & forever, the embodiment of Womanism…You live still… Rest in Power & Peace!

ACKNOWLEDGMENTS

"Womanist is to Feminist
as purple is to lavender." ~ Alice Walker
Thank you for getting us hip — ✊🏿 😊 💜

I acknowledge that I need to rest more & have more fun.

I acknowledge that I am water…

THE BREATHS...

PREFACE
INTRODUCTION

LOVE *-24*

- 1. sweet potato pie *-25*
- 2. the shits *-26*
- 3. unrequited *-27*
- 4. octave *-28*
- 5. plastic fruit *-29*
- 6. 5 times *-30*
- 7. song *-31*
- 8. thunderstorm *-32*
- 9. time *-33*
- 10. murmur *-34*
- 11. fighting sleep *-35*
- 12. the dance *-36*
- 13. jazz *-37*
- 14. candy *-38*

- 15. cackle *-39*
- 16. little ones *-40*
- 17. libra moans *-41*
- 18. too bad *-42*
- 19. vibe too high *-43*
- 20. it's too late *-44*

BODY *-45*

- 21. womb *-46*
- 22. sacred places *-47*
- 23. pussy power *-48*
- 24. souls window *-49*
- 25. spaces *-50*
- 26. temple *-51*
- 27. perspire *-52*
- 28. breathe *-53*
- 29. flagellant *-54*
- 30. curses *-55*
- 31. right brain *-56*

- 32. pusher (heart) *-57*
- 33. run *-58*
- 34. ashy *-59*
- 35. blessings *-60*
- 36. sprint *-61*
- 37. left brain *-62*
- 38. eat *-63*
- 39. walk *-64*
- 40. shit *-65*

SOUL *-66*

- 41. chakra dance *-67*
- 42. memory *-68*
- 43. timeless *-69*
- 44. speck *-70*
- 45. knowing *-71*
- 46. intuitive *-72*
- 47. always been *-73*
- 48. soul speaks *-74*

- 49. whispers -75
- 50. safe -76
- 51. SOURCE -77
- 52. give and take -78
- 53. forever -79
- 54. travel -80
- 55. once before -81
- 56. truth teller -82
- 57. weary -83
- 58. steady -84
- 59. same ole' -85
- 60. soul cry -86

SPIRIT -87

- 61. the listening -88
- 62. every moment -89
- 63. guide -90
- 64. SHE is -91
- 65. CREATOR -92

- 66. warmth *-93*
- 67. completion *-94*
- 68. presence *-95*
- 69. YESHUA *-96*
- 70. in the cool *-97*
- 71. prayer *-98*
- 72. being *-99*
- 73. comfort *-100*
- 74. winds of G-D *-101*
- 75. the heat *-102*
- 76. going forth *-103*
- 77. nudges *-104*
- 78. visionary *-105*
- 79. warnings *-106*
- 80. miracles *-107*

HEARTACHE *-108*

- 81. she's gone *-109*
- 82. 1 knee *-110*

- 83. torture -*111*
- 84. forsaken -*112*
- 85. lay down, die -*113*
- 86. abandoned -*114*
- 87. never, anymore -*115*
- 88. motherless -*116*
- 89. how could you? -*117*
- 90. cruel -*118*
- 91. invisible -*119*
- 92. BLACK Prez -*120*
- 93. elder-less -*121*
- 94. unacknowledged -*122*
- 95. no love -*123*
- 96. not looking -*124*
- 97. rug -*125*
- 98. stabs -*126*
- 99. hatred -*127*
- 100. my people -*128*

WISDOM *-129*

- 101. silence *-130*
- 102. waiting *-131*
- 103. attack *-132*
- 104. tongue bite *-133*
- 105. sustaining *-134*
- 106. let em' think *-135*
- 107. longevity *-136*
- 108. peace *-137*
- 109. joy *-138*
- 110. serenity *-139*
- 111. anti-love *-140*
- 112. time *-141*
- 113. pick up sticks *-142*
- 114. read damn it! *-143*
- 115. spirits *-144*
- 116. the whole *-145*
- 117. to the finish *-146*

- 118. me primary -*147*
- 119. waking -*148*
- 120. grimace -*149*

SEX & SENSUALITY -*150*

- 121. weight -*151*
- 122. rivers -*152*
- 123. explode -*153*
- 124. senses -*154*
- 125. cleanse -*155*
- 126. wet -*156*
- 127. sands -*157*
- 128. home place -*158*
- 129. configure -*159*
- 130. she -*160*
- 131. cemented -*161*
- 132. holy carnal -*162*
- 133. lusty -*163*
- 134. winds -*164*

- 135. prayers *-165*
- 136. healer matrix *-166*
- 137. potions *-167*
- 138. make an us *-168*
- 139. giver, taker *-169*
- 140. replenish *-170*

CHILDREN *-171*

- 141. laughter *-172*
- 142. fear known *-173*
- 143. scrapes *-174*
- 144. like outside *-175*
- 145. harness *-176*
- 146. cloned essence *-177*
- 147. ancient *-178*
- 148. first thought *-179*
- 149. simple perfection *-180*
- 150. best wisdom *-181*
- 151. lil' toes *-182*

- 152. dead eyes -*183*
- 153. play is truth -*184*
- 154. no more free -*185*
- 155. watch me -*186*
- 156. scared to tell -*187*
- 157. lost -*188*
- 158. switch -*189*
- 159. sensitive fire -*190*
- 160. trustful -*191*
- **DEATH** -*192*
- 161. taps -*193*
- 162. rattle -*194*
- 163. 2 days before -*195*
- 164. eyes set -*196*
- 165. ready -*197*
- 166. 9 lives -*198*
- 167. uneasy flow -*199*
- 168. it's coming -*200*

- 169. next leg *-201*
- 170. shallow *-202*
- 171. cold earth *-203*
- 172. to prepare *-204*
- 173. flowers now *-205*
- 174. centered *-206*
- 175. how i want it *-207*
- 176. early flight *-208*
- 177. the decision *-209*
- 178. not ready *-210*
- 179. never know *-211*
- 180. transition *-212*

THE AFTERLIFE *-213*

- 181. thin air *-214*
- 182. chaperones *-215*
- 183. the journey *-216*
- 184. look who it is *-217*
- 185. conferences *-218*

- 186. life unending -*219*
- 187. resting -*220*
- 188. ancestral deliberation -*221*
- 189. growing, learning, ascending -*222*
- 190. far off memories -*223*
- 191. the big screen -*224*
- 192. to blow -*225*
- 193. best shape -*226*
- 194. getting it -*227*
- 195. wars -*228*
- 196. on duty -*229*
- 197. shaking -*230*
- 198. finality -231
- 199. tree of life -232
- 200. new beginnings -233

THANK YOU BEAUTIFUL ONES... -234
ALSO BY ORIT -235
AUTHOR BIOGRAPHY -236
NOTES -239

PREFACE

Womanish Breaths was inspired into existence by my own declaration as a *womanist,* and how beautiful and complete of a feeling I get from the word & all it encompasses. I feel womanism is big enough for all of my Divinity as BLACK & WOMAN with a soul; a speck of G-D... I have sworn off mainstream feminism, because it excludes BLACK Women and the struggles we face such as systematic racism & oppression, and *misogynoir.*

The term womanist/womanism was first coined by Alice Walker... It is a brand of woman-centered rights seeking and being, that is centered in BLACK Women's culture(s) and tradition(s). Womanism is warm and strong... I feel it addresses our needs throughly, and it includes various trains of thought that represent the nuanced & culturally diverse BLACK Women of the world. There is always space to expand in womanism, and as diverse BLACK Women continue to add to it; the more richer it becomes.

As BLACK Women of nuance, we do not have the same ideals of patriarchy, because our experience is vastly different and more oppressive, than that of white women. For many of us BLACK Women, we do not see white women differently from white men; when it comes to white supremacy. White men may have more pull than white women, but white women are directly in line, power wise that is, after white men…They have white privilege, and this makes many of them willfully blind, to BLACK Women's issues in mainstream feminism.

BLACK Women, for the most part, do not associate taking care of home, with being a slave to men, like many white feminists have expressed. BLACK Women are the strongest people on earth, who have had to work hard at the job, in the home, and around the community…We are capable of so much, and many of us love being career women, revolutionaries, and caretakers…We want not just BLACK women to be whole, but our BLACK men and children as well… And then the world by-proxy. After all, we are the literal originator of all humans. We want to get the *misogynoir* out of our communities, and be self-determining as individual women, and as members of our communities.

BLACK Women are bad ass women, with a strong propensity for intrinsic healer qualities… All of this is womanism, and all of this is a more accurate way of describing me, and many of my sisters… I am womanist.

INTRODUCTION

I am thrilled you are going to embark on this very special journey, of breaths from my womanist soul. I know this offering will fill you, and seem familiar, if you have been on the planet for a while… It's a work of love and life… And yes, I made this with BLACK Women in mind firstly… And as with all of my literary works, anyone with an open heart will be able to glean from its pages.

Each breath in this offering is between 137-140 characters… Micropoetry. Micropoetry was first introduced to me through my use of *Twitter*. I wanted to convey free verse poetic thoughts, and therefore, began developing this unique skill. As I began to explore micropoetry more in depth, I found that others were also using the micropoem as a powerful poetic expression, both online and offline.

Micropoetry is a powerful way to relay poignant truths; perfect for sharing my inhalations & exhalations. I hope that *Womanish Breaths* will replenish, heal, educate, and encourage you to embark on your own personal journey, of deeper truth-telling and self discovery. I am also very pleased to be adding to Womanist Literature, which is very important as we all map out our way, and leave a trail for others to follow when they need it…
So, are you ready to get started? Let's begin!

LOVE

1.
sweet potato pie

in your warm scent
mellow vibes tango
to the beat of feet
hitting carpet firm
welcoming, serving
loving— steadily sweet
true home, my heart

2.
the shits

disturbingly patient
waiting weeks unending
torture my food
longing my water
for your ringtone
alerting my soul
my gut…
will he finally?

3.
unrequited

comparison to
ocean depth is
bromide & undone
soul deep, infinite
capacity circular
but it's not me
that you see
that you crave
& I waste

4.
octave

i am water &
the oil you are
makes the Light
i reflect glimmer
& we don't mix
homestead is
our muddle
of time & desire
fate jests
& we laugh

5.
plastic fruit

perfect flaws
entombed by
sacrifice
slowly rotting
no air for soul
i match your fester
then Oya blows
i wake
walk away
i love me
you don't

6.
5 times

your love
full grown
but i no longer
felt rhythmic
in your melody
i felt sorry
'til your confession
of spasmodic dick
became my liberation

7.
song

knowing place
where notes
brush over words
appearing on their own
my tone atones
ancestral & present
colliding in future
in the key of life

8.
thunderstorm

nothing more truthful
to the lost parts of soul
than roaring cadence
dripping waters cool
light filling the skies
jazz seen
heart realized

9.
time

we have all the
time in the universe
& everything can
change at
any moment
& we'll always
be in some form
so our love will
find us again

10.
murmur

i've painted over
the graffiti
your selfish
soul left on my
heart chambers
i grab my chest
when it regulates
my remembrance
that i'm ok now

11.
fighting sleep

pretending i was
working — hiding
the crunchy dead leaves
in my throat--trying
to remember who i am
quickly or else
he'll know
i was waiting

12.
the dance

a prayer
making G-D
remember breaths
we share…
1-2-3-4-5-6-7-8
truth drips
limbs stirring
soul free for
spirit flowing…
1-2-3-4-5-6-7-8

13.
jazz

chord hitting
the minor string
in my heart
so i can
release what's
most dear to me
flying so free
under invitation
to glimpse at
my own soul

14.
candy

i gave you candy
to make you stay
too sweet
for your taste
but you ate
contact high
flying loftily above
never reaching back
to grab my hand

15.
cackle

the sound was like
a bomb & it scared
all who heard
the devastation of
my souls thrusting
the winds of strength
i always blow
blew no more

16.
little ones

thought by now
sooner than later
but here i am at 33
& i have yet to feel
my womb enlarge
to welcome the
specks of G-D
who share my breaths

17.
libra moans

i try to quiet it
from reservoirs
celestially planted
deep within dark wonder
love awakens my dawn
loudly scales moan
in season
out season

18.
too bad

absolutely not
it's too bad
& what can i do
with you who could
reject such essential
parts of you?
only to be found
within my heart cadence

19.
vibe too high

won't let
pieces of me
i've hidden so long
breaking my wings
impeding my flight
re-weighed down
by your low vibe
feathering freedom
expanse

20.
it's too late

once blind
now i see
it hurt fully like
the dankest part
of hell imaginings
but it was protection
it was lessons
now it's too late
& i'm safe

BODY

21.
womb

mysterious universe
where souls arrive
where souls depart
destination earth
or back to twilight
when the Light
detours...
never ends
life

22.
sacred places

allow anyone
in sacred places
& it will teach
hard way learned
how desecrating
holy obelisks & temples
demotes divinity
from deity to fetish

23.
pussy power

i got the power
the power, power
sis, you got the power
the power, power
can't let no man body
tell our pussies
how to thrive
we decide!

24.
souls window

few dare look
really look
into my eyes
'cause if you think
my words are
too strong
my truth
too sassed
don't dare look
in my eyes
i see you

25.
spaces

architecture refined
each arm & leg
spaces... between them
between my eyes--
length between my
belly & my thighs...
spaces that hold
eternal

26.
temple

to worship at
this alter
first offer
the tenderest
part of your soul
then you may lift up
your sacrifice
& if i'm pleased
you'll be blessed

27.
perspire

glistening
temperature high
body is cooling
so needed
yet we view it
mostly seen
shallowly
sexy or not
gross or hot
every drop
life or death

28.
breathe

breaths stutter now
not as sure as they
once were — struggle
yeah, i struggle to
bring air in fully
'cause i hold my breath
when i'm afraid

29.
flagellant

'cause pockets of
air get blown everywhere
inside our shell home
& things get stuck
we need release
or else we languish
we break wind
& live

30.
curses

she carried it from
her momma
it skipped her
now the odds fall on me
but i'm free 'cause
i sought wisdom
rejecting the curse spoken
& i live

31.
right brain

there is no time frame
even though
there really is
because getting soul
to whisper out of art
in ways--
that initiate change...
my only goal

32.
pusher (heart)

keep going & going
going steady
dutifully steady
pushing always
day by day
hour by hour
until it's time...
i will live on
only it will die

33.
run

gazelle like glide
long ass stride
carrying me further
places & destinations
to teams & dreams
& then one injury
takes away
my love
no more

34.
ashy

i shutter to realize
that my feet are as
ashy as the soul of
amerikkkan lies
'cause i was rushing
didn't take time
to moisturize...
shit!

35.
blessings

never been that serious
a sprain but not broken
a growth but not malignant
no hospitalization
very few cold & flu
good health abundant
grace

36.
sprint

it's not the feel
of the pat-pat-pat
that makes my heart
sing melodically
but the vanity of
winning--basking
in the win is why i
pat-pat-pat

37.
left brain

positioned against
the carefree in me
soul escape
i plan & i gaze
& gaze to be sure
it's just so
every detail known
but soul says
never mind

38.
eat

it use to be because
i was famished &
then it was because
i wanted a bigger ass
but now it's neither
now i partake only
of what keeps my
glo

39.
walk

in the cool of the day
i follow the steps of
others 'cause i've
slowed down my pace
& in that flow i realize
time & space
made me right now

40.
shit

not just anywhere
oh no, i gotta wait
i need solace to relax
not wonder if you hear
if you smell--
recognize my shoes?
hell nah!
i'll wait

SOUL

41.
chakra dance

light beam, up down
align move over
side to side
inhale exhale
mindful & ready to
supplant negative energy…
become
more steadily
all of me

42.
memory

truth in form soars
& then a soul light
flickers, warming
my heart strings—
my fingers
play the melody
that i've always known
forever home

43.
timeless

glad my newer body
ain't reject my ancient soul
'cause old wine
in new wineskin
could break
the synchronicity
but blessed be SHE
it doesn't

44.
speck

I AM yes I AM
reflection
glimpse
a small part
of eternity
& completely filled
with divinity
I AM yes I AM
wholeheartedly
I AM
speck of G-D

45.
knowing

i spent time
so much time tuning
into my truest frequency
hearing the perfected me
in my soul stirring
this the beginning
truest of knowing

46.
intuitive

maybe she's born with it
& maybe
she's given keen sense
to see that
which alludes all
but EYE---traveling
to & fro... nothing
hidden
colors

47.
always been

continuance, no end
shadows shifting light
light remains still
& where i was, leave
& where i am, arrive
i've always been
always been alive

48.
soul speaks

every chamber
every life line
every organ
every gust
every low
every high
mutes moving
stilling
'cause when soul speaks
instruction begins

49.
whispers

ancestors
so many on hand
their word winds
their winds demands
for my good, my best
each cold cool breath
quietly sternly
leading me forth

50.
safe

YESHUA exemplified the
way to remembrance
& i am safe because
i am open to more
than what is written
& i don't limit so
i can grow
securest

51.
SOURCE

infinity is limiting
i beg pardon
being so undone
unable to capture
the magnificence
of all that YOU are
& YOU love me
to YOU i'll return

52.
give & take

was tired, tired
but i rolled up 'cause
you asked me to
i wanted to go back
to warm covers
& sleep but then
you blessed me
blessed me
me

53.
forever

i'll always have
to deal with me —
imperfections & my securities…
my rough spots & smooth as stone
complexities…
never ending
goddess

54.
travel

journey musta' been
rough 'cause
memory is shot
musta' rumbled
tumbled harsh
getting into a body
musta' been rough
& i don't remember shit!

55.
once before

wait, didn't i just...
see you here before?
i was here, right now...
but wait, was it a dream?
clash of impression
all that will be
known

56.
truth teller

bubbling forth
from my depths
eye think i could
only withhold
what's most real
to save a life
to save a soul
otherwise i must
keep it entire

57.
weary

so tired of saying
that i'm tired
because it does
nothing but parch
hope my enemy
truth my marriage
remembrance tryst
& still
love lifted me

58.
steady

the fluctuations
spirit trying to adjust
to turbulence on this
flight called life
ascend
descend
hydroplane onto souls'
sure & steady ground

59.
same ole'

nothing is new
i've hit this bump
a time before
but i forget--relearn
as if it's new
but it's simply not
so this time
will i learn
to rest?

60.
soul cry

i want freedom
i want babies
i want freedom
i want safety
i want freedom
i want justice
i want freedom
i want airy
i want freedom
i want me

SPIRIT

61.
the listening

pausing so that i
can tap into that
which took me
considerable time
to arrive & focus
sometimes i hold
my breathe so
that i can hear
visions

62.
every moment

a ting here
a nudge there
i ignore sometimes
seldom ever
because i know
tomorrows are in
the belly of
the obedience
of today--
safe passage

63.
guide

so long learning
to lean on---
lean on---
leaning on the
everlasting arms
so secure
these arms inside
i wouldn't survive
without its hold

64.
SHE is

SHE was
SHE is
always has been SHE
always been her, not he
SPIRIT of holiness
divine femininity of SOURCE
dwelling within--
always been — SHE

65.
CREATOR

& it's so wild how
i can come from
& be one with
everything
& yet only
scratching the surface —
that's wild!
i worship wildness
love is wild

66.
warmth

balmy breathes of
G-D blown anew
from the sacral
all the way--
explosion in soul
melting
frosty winter
in my mind
snowy mountain
in my heart

67.
completion

a rest
but when?
i don't know--
leaving this body
freeing soul
to go forth to
the next phase...
is it the last?
completion?
rest at last?

68.
presence

every hair stands
to challenge the
air to a duel
& i have no say
because entranced, i am
& fear speaks in my ear
a worthy
& glorious
terror

69.
YESHUA

every road
every question
it always leads back--
leads back to you
'cause however you express
no matter the newness
of remembrance
it is you

70.
in the cool

it be like that
huh, GREAT ONE?
always
yang in ying
balance everything
teaching us
strategy & love
when to move
when to hush
cool of day

71.
prayer

every move & word
every intention & care
every time i dance
every time i swear
every time i climax
every time i breathe
high truth — answered

72.
being

getting where it's just
the state of being
a fully integrated
spiritual incarnation
first nature listening
whispers leading to
a home place

73.
comfort

when i don't even want
to feel the cool breeze
peace drying
my hot tears
salty burn
then it comes...
hyssop on my soul
& the light shifts

74.
winds of G-D

destructive in nature
everything gotta
be brand new--
sturdy dwelling
must erect where
ruins once stood
tempest blow
grind & shake
rebirth

75.
the heat

fire in my bones
in my soul
whether instruction
whether woe
i gotta move
i gotta do
everything stirring
the fire's burning
so i can finish

76.
going forth

i hate being obtuse
& that's exactly what
i'm called to do
i tried avoiding destiny
but it found me
brought a belt
& whipped my BLACK ass

77.
nudges

i don't have to
understand completely
mysteries make love
with destiny--
i am born
i grow & grow
& then know
each nudge
that i obey
propels

78.
visionary

knocked me out
'cause my brain
thinks it does
what only heart & soul
can actualize
so i can see
aerial views decisions
to warn, to pray

79.
warnings

twisted stomach
unease in the
everywhere's
'cause i know i need to stop
to not precede
& most times i'm grateful
& sometimes i roll my eyes

80.
miracles

i know G-D is...
'cause my reality has
always tiptoed the divine
life has kicked my ass
but always
in the nick of time
i'm saved
still here

HEARTACHE

81.
she's gone

at first they tried
to lie & say...
that you hadn't flown
so i threw a fit trying
to get to the room
i imagined you in
but you weren't there

82.
1 knee

i had a dream
& it alerted me
you were way worse
then i could imagine
so i sleuthed online
saw you on one knee
proposing to her
& not to me

83.
torture

stuck in the haze
of stokholm & fear
no inward capacity
to escape hell
choosing survival
pretending it's ok
my guilt & shame
of daily rape

84.
forsaken

gave everything up
for what you said
i trusted that
i wouldn't
be shamed
i'm here
the experiences
auto-replay
trying to forget
& heal

85.
lay down, die

for us BLACK deities
just trying to breathe
always hindered--
cops thirst blood
do we submit...
or keep our dignity?
either way
no guarantee

86.
abandoned

no matter
how old or young
if ever the one
who gives birth
decides she's done
& letting her be
cease chasing dreams
of what she can never be

87.
never, anymore

i knew this was it
i cried hot tears
'cause she threw another fit
& for what?
then SPIRIT said: hush!
"i'm breaking the ties
it's done!"

88.
motherless

when you were around
i never felt i was from you
felt your love rarely
to the point it
became toxic
i shall not want
& still, i love you

89.
how could you?

always talking
about how much you
love G-D--celibate
so i believed your lies
but you were playing
me for a fool
so karma says:
she got you!

90.
cruel

white folks come
on twitter to laugh
when BLACK Folks
meet their death from
killer cop demons
i'll never get why
sadism feeds
their apathy

91.
invisible

i'm not trying to be a
household name
fighting for our freedom
but the disrespect is epic
i'm always serving--
but does my BLACK ass matter?

92.
BLACK prez

too many mesmerized
by swag & faux AAVE
annoying my souls soul
& while everyone gets
a good kee-kee
our people are set up
still we're dying

93.
elder-less

i now don't feel
as bad as i did
realizing
that every older
is not an elder
still i know
that we can't
make it forward
without you--
weep...

94.
unacknowledged

i was a fool to allow
you to hold me
tightly grasped
fuck you soul-less
like mine wasn't parched
all of me you wanted
none of me worshipped

95.
no love

there's been times
where no one on earth
loved me...
i became a well
empty & deep
crying fresh waters
filling myself up
drinking
refreshed

96.
not looking

they'll have to find me
whomever gonna
send me swangin'
'cause heartbreak has
stabilized my bio clock
& my lonely nights--
all or nothing

97.
rug

not even respectful
enough to wipe
your dirty feet
off the beautifully
designed rug that
i became for you
misunderstanding--
a profane love

98.
stabs

it will never fail
in this life
to feel the stabs
at least once--
giving big &
being repaid by
hatred & discord
extra heavy burden
to bear

99.
hatred

race hatred is
so great a woe
systematic in nature
global in appearance
it suffocates
it maims
it destroys
it kills...
laughing as we die

100.
my people

it breaks my heart
in millions of pieces
that BLACK people
my people
have lost so much
struggle so hard
unable to see
we are our best thing

WISDOM

101.
silence

warmth moves from
my chest down
to my cheeks...
can you see steam...
coming out my ears?
i heed the inward hush
beckoning the greater good

102.
waiting

patience is the virtue
attained & those
truly acquainted
never boast
because it's path is
a rocky road of pain
tred bare
injured sole
soul

103.
attack

when right winds blow
& the sun leads time...
moon aligning season...
i aim at my target
& fire
in quick succession
i fire---
til' bullseye

104.
tongue bite

& i really want to
gift you with a portion
of my lucidity
but my soul
says hush...
blessings coming--
can't let
them drown in
petty streams

105.
sustaining

is it worth it?
debasing my humanness
to survive evil eye--
cop terror
is it worth it?
diminishing goddess
to sustain breath?
no guarantees

106.
let em' think

i've concluded that
it's ok to let em' think
that i'm not one who matters
'cause eyes off me
gives me more space
to produce genius
unmatched

107.
longevity

move in truth
listen & heed
take only what's yours
give only what's meant to be
it won't be easy
it won't always feel good
karmic investment

108.
peace

what is peace
that doesn't last?
--that can only be
inwardly realized
while outwardly banned...
what is peace
it doesn't last--
is it real?

109.
joy

folks understand but
it takes overstanding--
to realize that joy isn't a given
for everybody...
some will never know
~home~
some will never

110.
serenity

i don't
know a lot about
the good feelings--
still waiting for life
to be kind to me...
but i'm traveling
the right road--
this my comfort

111.
anti-love

i don't want it
i don't need it--
love that is not real
love that does not care
love that does not move
you or he or she to ask:
are you ok?

112.
time

we don't have enough time
& yet we have eternity
so best to follow
soul whispers
& heart cadence steady
being ready to shift
& become
again

113.
pick up sticks

the key is to make
moves without disturbing
the flow of others--
gain momentum
adding to your stack
without displacing
those playing along

114.
read damn it!

ain't no got' damn
such a thing
as being informed
& refusing to read...
for fear of reality--
a dead end
& no...
i won't ride
in this wagon

115.
spirits

paying my respects
by first acknowledging--
i am not my own
there is more to learn
more to realize
manifestations
oneness
broadening scope

116.
the whole

all or nothing
'cause my soul is
tired of compromise
why is it " too much"
for me to say--
we deserve more?
why is it radical to love truth?

117.
to the finish

i do what i gotta'
to make my
procrastination obey
my goals & dreams
& i set rigid rules
for me, by me
no excuses
libra or not
here i come

118.
me primary

bold colors
all the lively ones
colliding to make a
unique hue--liquified
in refiners fire blaze
allowing the settling in:
i stain this life

119.
waking

when still sleepy
i'd roll back over
press the snooze button
again & again
but then
i realized
rousing myself
allows me to
welcome the dawn

120.
grimace

i oft don't even realize
'cause i hardly smile--
when i do
it's so foreign
& it literally makes
my face ache--
pain transplanted
from soul

SEX & SENSUALITY

121.
weight

i love your heavy
but only when
face to face
soul to soul
smothered under you
a danger i risk gladly
penetrated by you
an ecstasy i return

122.
rivers

pure waters from
holy space where
human kind worships--
rivers flow
yes flow...
baptizing sacrifices
& offerings laid bare
ecstasy purified

123.
explode

it's a taste of what
we have forgotten
a glimmer of our
most divine nature
when orgasming--cum
a spiritual episode
memories
relic eternal

124.
senses

nose ain't just to smell
tongue ain't just to taste
ears ain't just to hear moans
hands ain't just to caress
eyes ain't just to see you…

125.
cleanse

be careful of who bows
in your sacred grove--
who walks & picks
your choicest fruit
if by chance
the wrong one enters
purge them out
& lock

126.
wet

it's like the key
to my secret garden
causing the door to
open easily & wide
sweetly scented resin
of honey oshun
upon the petals
of my rose

127.
sands

'cause it was so good
baby fucked me sleep
my ritual for after
misplaced...
i awake hazy
was it a dream?
then the sands
remind me
it was so

128.
home place

not uncomfortable
'cause it's home
doesn't feel forced
'cause it's home
doesn't hurt
'cause it's home
no beginning or end
'cause we're home

129.
configure

i've never done this--
a kinda awkward sexy
driving us thirsty
she gives than receives
she receives than gives
one vibe
one high
our groove

130.
she

the divine isn't as
much feminine as
the feminine is divine...
& this sensual energy
balanced with love
will heal everyone
who embraces it

131.
cemented

i am not to be separated
from my sexuality
from my sensuality
i need not be ashamed
i need not curb truth--
breaking chains
embracing holy

132.
holy carnal

& then i realized
G-D doesn't think
that my pussy is gross
that my vagina is shameful
that my yoni is sin inducing--
holy between my thighs

133.
lusty

lusty is a privilege
i have yet to afford
it can only be done right
when love & respect reign first
lusty is dangerous
with the wrong one

134.
winds

ancestors must have
brought us together...
winds like these
only known in dreams
yet it blows
so powerfully
i still feel it
when i come to—

135.
prayers

all sorts of different
ways to pray...
each important
each has purpose
& we oft don't realize
sensuality's supplication
communion with self

136.
healer matrix

marvin gaye tried
to get us hip &
for so long i missed
healing aspects
of sex & sensual
transforming--
essence of soul
reconciled forever's

137.
potions

don't need no potions
to reel you into me
my ori is intoxicating
my essence is captivating
can you handle me...
all of me truest?
we'll see

138.
make an us

intention is all
& when it's time
i'll let down my guard
& we'll merge our souls
in the light of my womb
a perfected piece
of me & you
awake

139.
giver, taker

distributing our pressure
so that we both get
what we need &
it's not equal 'cause
we have varied needs
but it's balanced
intuitive
& whole

140.
replenish

there's a fountain of
memories that we can
dip our toe in
from time to time
& we oft don't
realize divine self can
be hidden in lower
nature

CHILDREN

141.
laughter

healing sound
that can surely
correct every
malicious vibe--
if only we could amplify
their balming hysterics
then the world
could breathe

142.
fear known

for the BLACK child
it happens much sooner--
that time frame of
carefree & uncare
racism severing
for the BLACK child
some may never
recall

143.
scrapes

it was was like a
daily ritual--
so clumsy
they told me
so uncareful
it was said
& no one ever
considered that
long legs were
hard to manage

144.
like outside

baby you smell like
outside...
like running & biking
like the creek & cig smoke
from your bff's house...
like candy & must...
like freedom

145.
harness

no matter the boundaries
that society places on
our minds & souls
a child awakens us
to innate ability--
to escape things that
wish us plain

146.
cloned essence

will she or he
be just like me?
in pairs or solo
when will i meet you?
i long to greet you--
that part of my essence
locked up in your
being

147.
ancient

yes you are an old soul
yes baby, you've been here before--
& let's not just dismiss this
let's figure out why
you've come back
this perfect

148.
first thought

when we're kids
we trust our first thought
'cause we haven't learned
to second guess
& this is why the young
can hear
the ancestors
whisper

149.
simple perfection

look at you brown baby
personality brighter than
sun of a thousand days
dancing & keeping time
& can't even walk yet--
talkin' real good too

150.
best wisdom

listen to children
they hold wisdom pure
they hold un-jaded life
they can see the root
because they are so
close to the ground--
hear them

151.
lil' toes

i'm in awe when
i gaze at feet
so small... of a child
how active & lively
how determined & ready
those lil' toes carry
& will lead their way

152.
dead eyes

to see breaths stay
but life leave eyes--
a young one abused
horror untold
depth unknown
my soul dies...
resurrecting in
prayer
to give love

153.
play is truth

watch closely
listen intently 'cause
when children play
their make believe...
their storylines:
they determine
if we are doing
right by them

154.
no more free

sad is the day that
a child... any child
but especially
a black child--
sad is the day
they are aware
of the target
on their precious
backs

155.
watch me

aunt bea would always
watch me play--
so exciting for me
as i engaged in the park sand
she'd nod on in enjoyment
& in this i knew such love

156.
scared to tell

train up lil' ones
in ways that are true
& if ever they're harmed
they won't fear telling--
for safe passage
will meet them
& love will **act**

157.
lost

when tamir rice
was executed by cop
a few kids asked
if they were next--
i said: "no, of course not!"
my confidence lied
lost 'cause of loss

158.
switch

i dread my mom's
belt with gold studs
& aunt bea
never laid a hand...
in jest ms. sharon
threatened her
son & i
with tree limb
as we laughed

159.
sensitive fire

i could discern it all
ever since i can recall
it bothered me--deeply
yes, i had infernos stirring
in my tiny frame
& freedom chose
me early

160
trustful

never blindly trust
young one so sure
that you know everything
'cause not even adults do
but we know a bit more
please heed our no
know love

DEATH

161.
taps

the old folks say
that when there's
a knock at the door
& you open to air
that death was near
so say a prayer
& ask for health
for your home

162.
rattle

when they leave us...
it's such a busy transition
so much seen & unseen--
as soul is prepped for flight
body winds engine down
then silence

163.
2 days before

omens...
angels & ancestors
know & prepare--
2 days before she left me
lucky got loose
& pushed his way...
barking where she'd
breathe last

164.
eyes set

3 am
i was eleven
asleep on the couch
you hadn't made
me go to bed
'cause your new
journey started
eyes set my way
your goodbye note
of love

165.
ready

life has been so hard
there have been times
i've prayed to die
but a young girl
much less healthy
than i--she helped
me see i was
ungrateful

166.
9 lives

listen!
death has stalked me
a few times--eerily
to scare or taunt...
so i taunt back
with my presence
plenty work left
my time
not yet
up

167.
uneasy flow

for many who don't
die in sleep or crash...
dying is as complicated
as being born--
there are pains
there is struggle
letting go
isn't easy

168.
it's coming

for you
for me
it's coming--
death of
this shell
freeing soul & spirit...
well prepared
or caught off guard
it's coming
for you & me
one day

169.
next leg

when body stops
hoisting our ancient
then we will begin
a new leg of our journey
final stop eternity?
maybe this time
who knows
what's next?

170.
shallow

when earth which
we are comprised--
commands air to resign
from a form...
from a life...
lungs don't like waste
so it expresses
until
still

171.
cold earth

i'm always cold
anyone who loves
me will surely fret...
wondering if the
cool cold earth
is causing me distress
but worry not
i'm not there

172.
to prepare

is there a way
for the meticulous
part of my brain
to detail an escape...
where loved ones
won't fight or hate
each other--
is there a way?

173.
flowers now

imma be pissed
if y'all drape my lifeless form
in calla lily black stars--
flower i most adore...
so i gotta die to get em'?
that's fucked!

174.
centered

not a big fan of hope
but i "hope" i make it
to the center--
of my purpose
of my journey
of my understanding
why i'm here
centered = ready

175.
how i want it

in my sleep is
how i want to go
'cause i don't want
to struggle--
this life is extra hard as is
black woman disparaged--
so death be kind

176.
early flight

your gate number not
even showing yet
but you cut in line
& i get it--regretfully
but it's ok 'cause
with open arms
you were met
peacefully

177.
the decision

staying in a body
wrecked with pain
is weary on souls
& we...
our opinions ain't shit--
if the choice to free soul
is the choice that heals

178.
not ready

when i was close...
death milliseconds away
so it seemed...
it made me realize
i didn't want to die
i want to breathe
& fulfill my purpose

179.
never know

an old deacon
at my aunt bea's
church would say:
"get your house
in order!"--
~ashe'~
the path is short
so fix things now
time doesn't
wait

180.
transition

some say they've
tasted death
& came back--
this could be
yet my gut feel
is when it's time
to travel on
brand new
will the
experience be

THE AFTERLIFE

181.
thin air

i think sometimes
i forget at one time--
i thought that
the other realms didn't
collide as much
as they do...
that inner-sight
is conscious

182.
chaperones

the second realm
can overwhelm--
light & dark
fighting for control
intertwined struggle
our CREATOR knows
we'll never travel alone
fear not

183.
the journey

i imagine it's quite
the journey--
leaving earth
at the appointed time...
it's different
for each soul
just as it is
on this side
of life

184.
look who it is

my mind is limited...
me seeing the one who
loves me best?
finally no more chasm
between us?
no more distance?
oh, i can't imagine...
joy!

185.
conferences

can't wait to see
how it's set up
especially during
times when the
ancestors meet
will i get to listen in?
will they want to hear from me?

186.
life unending

there is eternal
there are judgments
there are levels...
& what we do now
it matters...
& who knows when
or if we'll ever end
our traveling

187.
resting

what does rest mean
when not in earth restriction?
when pain has passed
& struggle is distant memory?
ah, maybe that is it--
that is rest!

188.
ancestral deliberation

try to imagine our
ancestors at their best
try to understand that
they have grown wiser
tap into that wisdom--
don't limit who
they are now

189.
growing, learning, ascending

there are levels
upon levels &
very few of us
will get the clue
of how much we
don't know &
how much we'll grow
levels to
ancestral breaths

190.
far off memories

our memory
softly deleted
remnants remain--
but fragmented...
before we
traveled through
our mother's
G-DDess...
so we could learn
humility

191.
the big screen

when it's all
said & done
will you be proud
of your featured film...
or will you be shamed?
what's your truth?
there is still time--
change

192.
to blow

i wonder what
it is like
to be able to
add to the gusts...
to be assigned to
work with strong winds--
everything done precise
or else...

193.
best shape

a fat ass & small waist
ain't got nothing on
the perfection of
your soul shape--
if you take care
& nurture it
that is...
allowing it true

194.
getting it

i wonder if i'll
be told that
i finally "got it"--
whatever it is
whatever it was
whatever it will be
did i finally get it?
did i finally?

195.
wars

there will be wars
like we have never seen
& it will turn all
of earths time
into a continuation
of eternity...
ushering us into
true peace

196.
on duty

i have work to do
& it will always last
so let me get
my shit together
so i can be best prepared--
prepared for this work
soul's always done

197.
shaking

wiped out like
an etch a sketch
it's going down--
whether ancestor or
still tied to earth laws...
we'll all become free
newness will
emerge

198.
finality

this has been
a long tedious run
of a complicated
stage play
& we've all been
exposed for what
we truly are--
end scene...
new act begins

199.
tree of life

there is healing for
the nations
in fruit
we can not yet eat--
& our perceptions
will change...
we'll be glorious
non-human beings
ascending

200.
new beginnings

what if we ascend to
our highest selves
for what we think is
a permanent state...
but then find out
we have to do this shit
all over again?

Thank You Beautiful Ones…

… For taking the time to inhale and exhale with me. I hope that this offering has touched you in ways that heal, that are familiar, that are comforting, that are hilarious, and that are uncomfortable… Yes, uncomfortable is good! As long as it was true for you, I am glad that you felt it… I am glad that you shared air with me.

Please take time to revisit any of the 200 breaths that gave you pause, that especially touched your being, or that made you feel something deeply for some other reason. Explore "the why's" and how you can grow from those tugging's.

May blessings, growth, new paths, and newness in every way be yours.

In Unashamed Négritude & Revolutionary Love,

ORIT

Also By ORIT...

Available at
amazon.com

For More Info Visit: WWW.ORITVIBES.COM

Author Bio

ORIT is a Lover of G-D/ Freedom Fighter/ Poet/ Wordsmith/Healer/ Performing Artist (Singer-Actress-Dancer)/ Sarcasm Connoisseur/ Humor Enthusiast/ among many other things.Uniquely of Pan-African (African-American and Ethiopian Jewish) descent, ORIT grew up in a small city in South Central Ohio, USA.

After many years of cultivating experiences and travels all over, ORIT moved back to Ohio in recent times, and now resides outside of Columbus. ORIT has been using words in every way possible to communicate messages since childhood. She not only writes them, but she is also a Multi-Lingual Orator and Spoken Word Artist, who can rouse & puncture hearts skillfully... When she wants to, that is…

ORIT is a very down to earth person, and prefers using common & authentic language to communicate in ways, that reminds everyone to level out ego, and embrace the hearth of the message. ORIT believes that the words, though important in there choosing, are only a reflection of the message...

"What a person remembers most will be what they take from your over all vibe as you speak words... The messages they decode from the unspoken weigh heavy... Did I convey the message wholly?"
~ ORIT

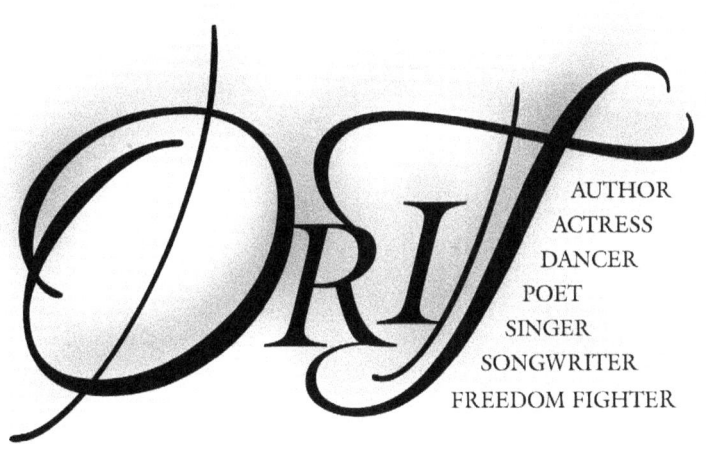

NOTES

www.ingramcontent.com/pod-product-compliance
Lightning Source LLC
Chambersburg PA
CBHW070548050426
42450CB00011B/2763